CONTENTS

INTRODUCTION

The astonishing new technology in contemporary textiles is narrowing the gap between the worlds of art, design, engineering and science. The use of 'flexible' materials is increasing as solutions are sought for a whole variety of specialist needs. The inherent characteristics of the new textiles underpin the functional and aesthetic qualities of their many and various applications from the world of fashion to architecture.

Part I opens with the chapter on 'Future Fibres and Fabrics' which discusses microfibres that are being specifically engineered at a molecular level in the world's most advanced laboratories. A whole new range of looks and performance characteristics are being created. The fibres are tough, hard-wearing and resistant to many chemicals, and also present us with new aesthetics that are proving very desirable. Fabrics made from these new fibres are judged on their own merits, unlike the early synthetics which were seen as cheap alternatives to luxury fabrics such as silk. The new pliant materials are also examined. Particularly interesting is the way that metals are being used in combination with textile techniques to provide very versatile fabric structures. The fibres and fabrics introduced here are the key to the future.

The chapter on 'Electronic Textiles' looks at the influence of the computer on textiles and at wearable technology. Computer Aided Design (CAD) has revolutionized the design process, introducing a sense of three-dimensional space into two-dimensional design, bringing with it a whole new visual aesthetic. The chapter's main focus is on the influence of the cyborg on clothing. The term cyborg was coined by Manfred E. Clynes and Nathan S. Kline to describe an enhanced human being who would be able to adapt to living in an extra-terrestrial environment. The concept has influenced the design of spacesuits as well as wearable mechanisms, improving our communication with each other and with our environment. Many of these designs incorporate external devices which act as a prosthetic enhancement of our senses.

'Engineered Textiles' begins with a look at many of the lightweight, hybrid materials that are starting to replace heavier materials. These are part-textile (flexible), part-non-textile (glass, metal, carbon and ceramic). Alongside these developments are three-dimensional construction processes which make it possible to reduce both the number of production stages and the wastage of material. This chapter also discusses composites, non-wovens and geosynthetics. Composites are, by definition, the combination of two or more materials that differ in form or composition in order to create a new material with enhanced performance characteristics. Non-wovens include a number of different processes in which the fibres are directionally or randomly orientated. Geosynthetics is the term for most porous flexible materials that are used in or on soil, and includes a range of grids, nets and meshes.

Several of the many exciting developments in the finishing of textiles are examined in the chapter on 'Finishes'. A fabric can be completely transformed in colour, texture and form at the finishing stage, and

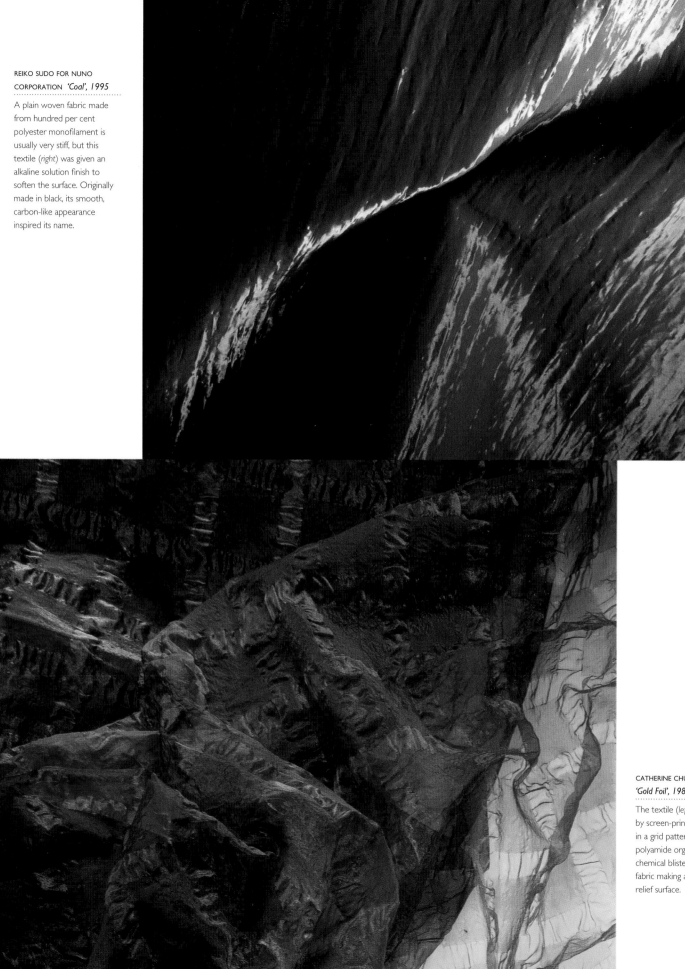

REIKO SUDO FOR NUNO CORPORATION *'Coal', 1995*

A plain woven fabric made from hundred per cent polyester monofilament is usually very stiff, but this textile (*right*) was given an alkaline solution finish to soften the surface. Originally made in black, its smooth, carbon-like appearance inspired its name.

CATHERINE CHUEN-FANG LEE *'Gold Foil', 1987*

The textile (*left*) was created by screen-printing chemicals in a grid pattern on shot polyamide organza. The chemical blisters the synthetic fabric making an attractive relief surface.

JEAN-PAUL GAULTIER
Autumn/Winter 1996/97
Collection
....
Many leading fashion
designers love the look of the
latest synthetics. The Eastern-
inspired asymmetric cut
(*below*) is given a twist by
the choice of fabric – a shiny
synthetic like a second skin.

OWEN GASTER *Spring/Summer*
1996 Collection
....
Owen Gaster combines
classic British tailoring with
experimental materials.
Transparent layers create
a shimmering vest top worn
over trousers made of a
sleek textile with a high
sheen (*above*).

MARIANNE KOOIMANS
'Bubble Skirt', Spring 1995
....
The volume which can be
achieved by heat-setting the
fabric (*below*), thirty-seven
polyamide, sixty-three per
cent polyester, is used to
create a tulip-shaped skirt
which is contrasted with a
tailored jacket.

MARIANNE KOOIMANS
'Long Dress/Puffed Sleeves',
Spring 1995
....
Marianne Kooimans heat-sets
pure synthetics, thirty-seven
per cent polyamide, sixty-
three per cent polyester,
into striking configurations.
The line of the dress (*above*)
is emphasized by the vertical
pattern of the heat-set
iridescent fabric. The sleeves
are made from the fabric
in its original state.

industrial methods to produce designs that look hand-woven. The fabrics are unique and innovative, with a quality superior to most mass-produced fabrics. A subtle beauty and neutral colours are characteristic of Nuno textiles. They use diverse materials, such as metals and papers in combination with silks and polyesters. Layered-weave structures constructed on computer-assisted Jacquard looms are used for complex surface treatments and reversible fabrics. Making clothes from Nuno textiles demands skill, as the garment should not compete with the fabric. Loose, simple silhouettes and designs draped around the body rather than cut to fit display the fabric to the full. The designer Sayuri Shioda contributes both textiles and ideas for the small selection of clothes in Nuno's Tokyo shop.

These garments do not follow current fashion trends but are timeless and classic in their appeal.

Sophie Roet, working predominantly in the fashion world, is a freelance textile designer in Paris and London, and has created textiles for many fashion designers, including Romeo Gigli and Hussein Chalayan. Many of her textiles are fragile, developed for the fashion catwalk and not for everyday wear.

Textile design duo Mark Eley and Wakako Kishimoto formed Eley Kishimoto in 1992, and are

ELEY KISHIMOTO/JOE CASELY-HAYFORD *'Sun Print'*, *Spring/Summer 1995*

For fashion designer Joe Casely-Hayford, Eley Kishimoto coated a cotton and silk blended fabric with a collatype photographic solution of silver nitrate. With leaves in position, the fabric was exposed to sunlight, leaving leaf prints (*above*).

REBECCA EARLEY *'Electric Fence', March 1996, for Autumn/Winter 1996/97*

A stretched print, achieved with a metal heat photogram on polyester satin microfibre from the 'Be Earley' collection (*right*). The latest microfibres are ideal for this unique technique because they take the print well and it remains permanent even when machine washed.

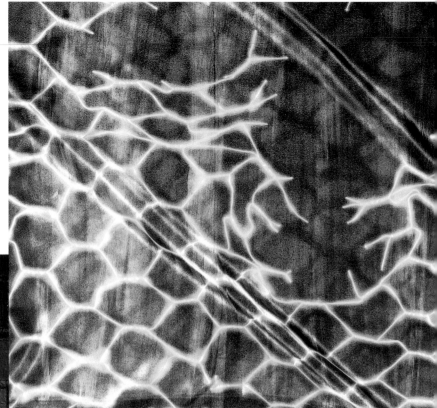

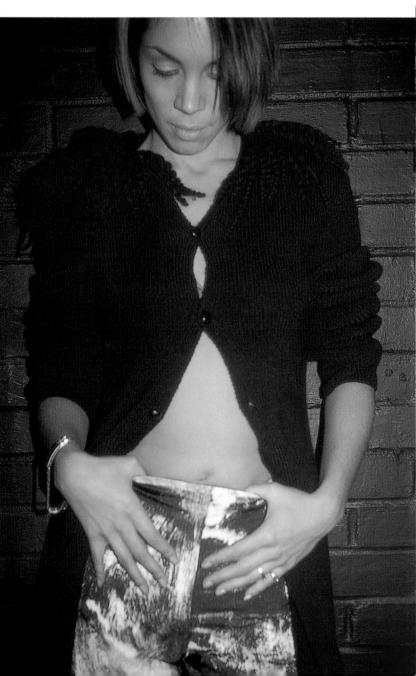

REBECCA EARLEY/GIOVANNA PALMIERO *'Retroflective Hand Printed Trousers', Duel Collection, March 1996*

A high-quality microfibre from the French company Sofileta was hand-painted first with retroflective ink made by Reflective Technology Industries Ltd in Manchester. Black ink was then added, and the fabric was fixed in a heat press, producing the effect of antique metal (*left*).

based in London. They use the latest fabrics and printing technologies, working to commission for fashion designers such as Donna Karan, Hussein Chalayan, Sonja Nuttall and Joe Casely-Hayford. Their own Autumn/Winter 1996/97 Collection showed clothes in innovative and functional fabrics, including polyurethane-coated silks and breathable polyamide for rainwear.

Rebecca Earley designs original textiles for fashion, and her work demonstrates that in the 1990s new technology is exploited not only for the materials and techniques but also for inspiration. She experiments with the latest microfibre fabrics combined with revolutionary methods of printing and newly-developed inks, including 'retroflective' ink. Unlike other reflective inks, this throws light back to its source, using a principle similar to that of the 'cat's eye' in roads. It is manufactured by Reflective Technology Industries Ltd, who make special tape for protective and safety clothing. Their technique is to suspend microscopic aluminium-coated glass spheres in the ink, which can be either oil or water-based making it suitable for a wide range of fabrics. It can

large clear span is needed, as in the Munich Ice Stadium. The structure of Nuage Léger at La Défense in Paris makes a feature of its cable supports, while the free edge of the membrane gives it a floating appearance. Conical forms are also popular and can be created by pushing or pulling with rings or reinforced areas. Umbrella structures are used in many outdoor sites to provide protection from the elements.

TEMPORARY AND MOBILE STRUCTURES

One of the most common designs for temporary or mobile structures consists of a series of aluminium portal frames between which fabric is stretched. Simplicity of erection and the robustness of the fabric are key design factors. Architects Apicella Associates, with Atelier One as engineers on the

project, have designed an ingenious system for the two-storey mobile Hong Kong Pavilion. The clients are the Hong Kong Tourist Authority who want to use the structure for promotion in up to fifty European cities. Two trailers use hydraulic lifts to level the chassis and raise the first floor frame. Floor panels open out to provide an atrium space. The aluminium frame bridges brace the two structural frames, while a double-skinned inflatable membrane forms the roof. The trailers are designed to be used in all weathers, and warm air is pumped in during winter months to prevent heat loss and condensation, with air conditioning and heating powered separately. Installation time was an important design consideration: it is estimated that the structure takes twenty-four hours to set up and is equally easy to dismantle.

J.O. SPRECKLESEN A/S WITH PAUL ANDREU/ADP: ARCHITECTS RFR/ OVE ARUP AND PARTNERS: ENGINEERS *'Nuage Léger', La Défense, Paris, 1984–89*

Visitors are often surprised by the scale of the 'light cloud' *(le nuage léger)* close up. From a distance it appears almost flimsy. The cable supports are made into a feature, while the free edge of the membrane makes it seem as if it is floating.

APICELLA ASSOCIATES: ARCHITECTS ATELIER ONE: ENGINEERS *Pavilion Hong Kong, 1994–95*

In this design for the Hong Kong Tourist Authority (*drawings opposite*), the aluminium frame is roofed by a double-skinned inflatable membrane. The combination of structure with means of transportation achieves economies of function and space.

KIYONORI KIKUTATE: ARCHITECT TENSYS: ENGINEERS *Resort Centre, Japan*

Woven glass fibres are coated with a fluoroplastic film, Hostaflon, for this transparent roofing membrane (*opposite right*).

MUF: ARCHITECTS *Purity and Tolerance, Installation at the Architectural Foundation, London, 1995*

Barrisol® Stretch Ceilings are commonly used as hygienic cover for kitchen ceilings or as reflective cover for swimming pools. Latex fabric, with a content of titanium for reflective qualities and strength, is stretched over the exposed concrete ceiling of the exhibition space. (*above*) A bulge created by water increases the reflective quality; it distends or contracts according to the body heat in the room because the fabric is responsive to temeprature.

SERGE FERRARI SA *Soltis screens, Banque Populaire de l'Ouest, Rennes, 1990*

Soltis membrane screens provide protection from the sun for the façade (*right*). Soltis, a fabric of high tenacity polyester coated with PVC, is made by Serge Ferrari SA.

NON-WOVEN Fabric with no formal structure, such as weave, knit or braiding. Instead the yarn is laid in a loose web before being bonded by heat, by adhesives, by high-pressure jets of water, or by needle-punching. With synthetics, heat and pressure are used to fuse the fibres. Non-wovens do not drape, stretch or fray and can be specifically engineered for different applications.

OBI Decorative stiff sash worn around the traditional Japanese kimono, constructed using complex Jacquard weaving.

ORGANIC SOLVENT SPINNING Organic solvents mix organic chemicals with water. Solvent spinning entails dissolving and spinning to obtain the fibre without any by-product.

PEAU DE PÊCHE From the French meaning 'skin of a peach', a sanded finishing technique applied to silk, popular in the late 1980s, which gently abrades a layer to give a soft feel and subtle colour.

PHENOLIC RESIN Thermosetting resin produced by an aromatic alcohol condensed with an aldehyde.

PILLING Balls of soft fibre formed by friction with the stronger fibre plied with it. These are trapped on the surface of the fabric by the stronger fibre. Blends of natural and synthetic yarns have a strong tendency to pill, but it can also happen with purely natural yarns. The only remedy is to 'shave' or comb off pilling. The prevention of pilling is under research. New microfibre blends seem to stay smooth despite constant wear.

PLY Fabrics or felts consisting of one or more layers, or number of fibres that make up a yarn, (such as 4-ply)

POLYESTER Thermoplastic fabric produced from the polymerization of ethylene glycol and dimethyl terephalate or terephthalic acid.

POLYETHYLENE Group of semicrystalline polymers mainly based on ethylene monomers

POLYMER Material formed by the chemical combination of monomers with either the same or different chemical compositions. Plastics, rubbers and textile fibres are examples of high-molecular-weight -polymers.

POLYPROPYLENE (PP) Semicrystalline thermoplastic textile.

POLYURETHANE Thermosetting resin prepared by the reaction of diisocyanates with polyols, polyamides, alkyd and polyether polymers.

POLYVINYL CHLORIDE (PVC) Polymerized from vinyl chloride monomers and compounded with plasticizers and other additives.

PREFORM Preshaped fibrous reinforcement formed by distribution of chopped fibres or cloth by air, water flotation or vacuum over the surface of a perforated screen to the approximate contour and thickness required. Used in the manufacture of composites.

PREPEG Ready-to-mould material in sheet form or ready-to-wind material in roving form, which can be cloth, mat, unidirectional fibre or paper impregnated with resin.

PULTRUSION Process by which fibre-reinforced material is pulled through a resin-impregnated bath and a shaping die where the resin is cured. This is a continuous process (see also extrusion).

REGENERATED 'Natural chemical' yarn from a natural source, such as wood pulp, chemically treated to create a new fibre. The first was viscose rayon and could be described as half natural and half synthetic. Different from pure synthetics, which are made from petrochemicals.

RESIN Solid, or pseudo-solid, organic material with the ability to flow when subjected to stress.

SANDING/SANDBLASTING Process of mechanically abrading fabric with a series of sandpaper covered rollers to remove the immediate surface layer of the fibres, making the fabric softer in feel, drape and colour.

SANDWICH CONSTRUCTION Composite made from a lightweight core material, such as honeycomb, foamed plastic, etc., to which two thin, dense, high strength or high stiffness skins are adhered

SASHIKO Traditional Japanese quilting for peasant wear. Formerly stiff in quality, and expensive. For general wear, uniforms and Japanese martial arts.

SHEARING Process giving a thermoplastic fabric a new form. On heating, the fibres shift, deform and take on a different shape when moulded. Critical factors include the size of the fibres and their spacing in the fabric construction.

SHIBORI Traditional Japanese resist-dye technique. Fabric is tied in a regular pattern stitched in place, then dyed and the stitches removed, resulting in a puckered appearance and a pattern formed from the areas of dyed and undyed fabric. The time-consuming technique is traditionally used for obi.

SHOT FABRIC Iridescent effect from using yarns of two different colours in a woven fabric, one in the warp and the other in the weft.

SIROSET Abbreviation of Commonwealth Scientific and Research Organisation describing a chemical treatment applied to wool in conjunction with hand pleating to fix permanent pleats. The bonds of the wool fibre are broken down, and a new structure is formed, which is fixed by pressing.

SLIT FILM Flat yarn made by cutting a sheet of material (usually synthetic) into fine slits.

SLUB Yarn that varies in thickness throughout its length. It has a fleecy core around which a finer yarn is twisted, highly twisted for thinness and loosely for thickness.

SOLARIZATION Photographic process by which a halo of light is produced around the subject when the print is exposed to light for a very short time before being completely fixed.

SPATTERING Technique for fixing very fine particles of metal, such as stainless steel, copper or titanium to a synthetic textile (the fabric must not contain water). Metals are broken down into microscopic particles in a vacuum using ionized argon gas and then fixed to the surface of the fabric. This happens at molecular level, and the finish remains permanent. The 'metal' fabric is fluid, and its texture is not altered by the thin coating.

SPUN BONDING Continuous or staple monofilaments are spun to form a sheet before being subjected to heat-pressurized rollers which weld the filaments together at their contact points.

STAPLE Short length of a fibre, also referred to as 'spun'. The most common natural staple yarn is wool. The shorter the staple length the more hairy and matt the yarn. The short fibres go in many directions making an uneven, broken texture. Synthetics can be produced in staple as well as filament yarns.

STITCH BONDING Process of bonding together fibres (particularly multifilaments) by stitching.

STRETCH In a 'warp stretch' the elasticity runs parallel to the selvedge of a woven textile. A 'weft stretch' runs horizontally from selvedge to selvedge. 'Bi-stretch' or 'two-way stretch' runs in both directions. A stretch fabric normally incorporates an elastic yarn, such as Lycra. Cutting a woven fabric on the bias, or diagonal, also imparts stretch. Knitted fabrics have natural stretch from their method of construction. Non-wovens do not stretch unless made from an elastic yarn.

SUBSTRATE Background or base to which a finish or treatment is applied

TAPA One of the oldest non-wovens, is made from beaten bark.

THERMAL BONDING Process of heat-bonding in which the outer surface of filaments is melted allowing crossover points to be fused together. Used for bonding polypropylene continuous filament..

THERMOPLASTIC Quality of a fibre whose molecular structure breaks down and becomes fluid at a certain temperature, making it possible to reshape the fabric by pleating, moulding, vacuum-forming or crushing. The fabric is 'fixed' on cooling and cannot be altered unless heated to a temperature greater than the one at which it was reshaped. Most synthetics are thermoplastic; of the natural textiles, wool possesses this characteristic.

THERMOSETTING POLYESTER Group of resins produced by dissolving unsaturated (generally linear) alkyd resins in a vinyl-type active monomer such as styrene.

TRILOBAL Rounded triangular cross-section of a fibre, which catches and reflects light.

TYVEK Tradename for spun-bonded olefin, a non-woven, paper-like material manufactured by DuPont, USA. Also known as 'envelope paper'. Strong, durable and resistant to most chemicals, originally developed for protective clothing, now also used for fashion.

ULTRA-VIOLET DEGRADATION Breakdown of fibres when exposed to sunlight.

VACUUM-FORMING Process by which plastic sheet film is heated to a liquid state, placed in a mould in a vacuum-former; all air is removed so that the plastic takes on the shape of the mould; this becomes permanent on cooling. Used for subtle relief textures or dramatic three-dimensional forms.

WARP Vertical threads fixed on the loom before weaving begins. A warp yarn needs to be strong and should not stretch.

WEAVING/WOVEN FABRIC Textile structure made by interlacing warp threads with weft threads. The three primary weave structures are plain, twill and satin.

WEFT Horizontal threads in a woven fabric. Weft yarn can be softer and weaker than the warp.

Abbreviated titles

Central St Martins: Central St Martins College of Art and Design, London
RCA: Royal College of Art, London
Goldsmiths' College: Goldsmiths' College, University of London
Winchester Sch. Art: Winchester School of Art

HELLE ABILD

Textile designer, born Denmark 1964.
Studied Textile Design, then Products and Furniture, Danmarks Designskole, Royal Academy of Fine Arts, Copenhagen. Freelance working in New York, San Francisco and London. Produced fashion collections for New York textile design studio Off the Wall, bridging the gap between fashion and textiles. Uses computers, scanning and manipulating images for fashion textiles.

AKZO NOBEL

Leading European manufacturer of technical textiles since 1930s.
Late 1970s began manufacture of non-woven textiles mainly for industrial and technical sectors, including carpets and geosynthetics. 1980s started production of aramid and carbon fibres. Manufacturer of Enka Viscose, and microfilament polyester fibres such as Diolen Micro for high-performance outdoor fabrics and for fashion. Research into high-tech membranes resulted in Sympatex, microfibre used as invisible weatherproofing laminate.

BIRGITTE APPLEYARD

Textile designer, born UK 1970.
BA Textile Design, Chelsea College of Art, London, specializing in Printed Textiles; MA Fashion, Central St Martins. Employed by Coats Viyella, sponsor of her graduation show, to design yarns for knit/weave market. Sells worldwide through London-based textile agency, Hodge & Sellers. Designs bought by leading fashion designers Calvin Klein and Giorgio Armani. Works for Donna Karan in New York.

JUN'ICHI ARAI

Textile planner, born Japan 1932.
Father wove fabrics for kimonos, grandfather a spinner. Birthplace Kiryú famous for Jacquard weaving and high-twist yarn production. Jun'ichi Arai has travelled in South America, India and Indonesia researching ancient textiles. 1950s pioneered new techniques working with metallic yarns in which he is considered an expert. 1970s, experimenting with computers. 1980s, exploring finishing techniques on synthetic textiles, including heat and chemical treatments. Set up first company Anthologie, working with plastics, synthetics and metallics as well as natural fibres. 1984 set up Nuno Corporation with Reiko Sudo, creating some

of the most exciting textiles for fashion and interiors ever seen. Designs use different characteristics of natural and synthetic fibres; experiments with every stage of construction and finishing, often exploiting thermoplastic quality of synthetics. One of the first to combine traditional Japanese techniques with sophisticated technology, using computers in both design and manufacture for Nuno, making very complex textures. Early 1980s, worked with Makiko Minagawa and Issey Miyake, and also supplied textiles for avant-garde fashion designers such as Comme des Garçons. Now works independently in Kiryú creating textiles for art works. There are thirty-six patents on his textiles. Has won many awards for elevating textiles to an art form. Work in many permanent collections, including Victoria and Albert Museum, London; Cooper-Hewitt Museum, New York. 1987 made Honorary Member of the Faculty of Royal Designers for Industry by the Royal Society of Arts in Great Britain. 1992 award from Textile Institute, UK.

HELEN ARCHER

Textile designer, born UK 1973.
1995 BA, Textile Design, Loughborough College of Art and Design, specializing in Printed Textiles. Uses techniques such as printing, embossing, and heat-treating textiles. 1995 at London's 'New Designers Show' showed her laminated textiles for interiors and fashion using holographic foils supplied by Astor Universal Ltd.

ASAHI CHEMICAL INDUSTRY

Leading supplier of synthetic fibres, based in Tokyo.
Products include polyamide, polyester and acrylic fibres. Developing new products, including electronic materials.

NIGEL ATKINSON

Textile designer, born UK 1964.
1986 BA, Textile Design, Winchester Sch. Art, specializing in Printed Textiles. Uses a printing technique to transform two-dimensional surface into relief texture that responds to light. Has own line as textile designer using both natural and synthetic fabrics. Supplies textiles to fashion designers such as Romeo Gigli and Alberta Ferretti. Has created fabrics for costumes for UK's Royal Shakespeare Company and National Theatre. Work to be found at A la Mode and Browns in London, at Takashimaya, and Saks Fifth Avenue, New York. 1996 sole textile designer representing Britain in Florence Biennale. 1997 set up Nigel Atkinson Interior Textiles.

SHARON BAURLEY

Textile designer, born UK 1968.
1986 BA Printed Textiles, Winchester Sch. Art.
1997 PhD, RCA, on technological and pictorial

ways of producing three-dimensional effects on fabrics. Also exploring thermoplastic properties of synthetics to make three-dimensional forms for interiors or fashion. March–April 1995 exhibited in 'New Techstyles', Nottingham. 1995–96 researched Japanese textile industry, particularly finishes, financed by Leverhulme Trust.

MARIA BLAISSE

Textile designer, born Netherlands 1944.
Studied Textile Design, Gerrit Rietveld Academy, Amsterdam. Worked in Jack Lenor Larsen Design Studio in New York. Travelled in South America studying indigenous crafts, including natural dyeing of fibres. 1974–87 Professor in Textile and Flexible Design, Gerrit Rietveld Academy. Since 1982 guest lecturer in colleges in France, Germany, Italy, UK and USA; also researching fibre engineering, rubber laminates, non-wovens and synthetic foams, creating unusual forms for fashion accessories and dance costumes. Employs vacuum-forming and laminating techniques to exploit thermoplastic nature of synthetics. Invited by Issey Miyake to create hats for his Spring/Summer 1988 Collection. Established Flexible Design in Amsterdam. Her work is important in its exploration of new materials and the crossover between the worlds of engineering, industry, textiles, fashion and art.

PHILIPPA BROCK

Textile designer, born UK.
Studied Textiles at Goldsmiths' College, specializing in Printed Textiles. Researched Computer Aided Design, particularly Jacquard fabrics, RCA. Further research into Jacquard weaving, University of Huddersfield. Worked as freelance textile designer selling samples through an agency for interior fabrics and more recently for fashion. Since 1994 Research Fellow in CAD/CAM Woven Textiles (Jacquard and shaft) at Winchester.

LIZA BRUCE

Fashion designer, born USA, based in London.
Clothes range from sportswear and swimwear to evening wear, uncluttered and contemporary in look.. Often uses latest synthetics blended with Lycra for body-conscious silhouettes.

LUISA CEVESE

Textile designer, born Italy.
Director of Research for Italian textile company Mantero Seta for many years. Set up own company making accessories from industrial waste material (often fabric selvedges) in combination with plastics. Also works for Mantero Seta liaising with art colleges in UK and France. Exhibited in Europe, Japan, UK and USA. Has made accessories for Barneys department store in New York, Bodyshop, Comme des Garçons and Paloma Picasso.

HUSSEIN CHALAYAN

Fashion designer, born Cyprus.
1993 graduated in Fashion, Central St Martins. Has shown many outstanding collections and established as important designer. Explores new textile materials, such as Tyvek and light-sensitive fabrics, for futuristic look. Icelandic singer Björk helped promote designs by wearing his clothes made from his paper fabrics. Attracted publicity when buried 'paper' garments with iron filings to distress with random rust markings.

TARUN CHAUHAN

Textile designer, born 1972, based in England.
1996 BA, Design Management, De Montfort University, Leicester. Freelance designer and consultant for several fashion companies such as Solo and New Star.

SIMON CLARKE

Textile artist, born UK 1963.
BA, Printed Textiles, Middlesex University; MA in Textiles, University of Central England. Investigated relationship between painting and printed textiles while Textile Fellow, University of Plymouth. 1991–93 Lecturer in Fine Art, Kenyatta University, Nairobi. 1996 appointed Senior Lecturer in Textile Design, Nene College of Higher Education, Northampton, and Visiting Lecturer in Textiles at Goldsmiths' College. Abstract textile art works influenced by Cornish and East African landscapes. Uses synthetic materials, such as Neoprene, and traditional materials, such as wool and silk, with heat-reactive dyes, metallic pigments, devoré and discharge processes. Exhibited in Cornwall and London.

DANIEL COOPER

Designer, born 1972, based in England.
1995 degree in Three-Dimensional Design, Leeds Metropolitan University; 1996 MSc, Industrial Design, University College, Salford. Has worked for both Daniel Poole and Paul Smith Ltd.

ANDRÉ COURRÈGES

Fashion designer, born France, 1923.
Trained, and worked for a time, as civil engineer. Apprenticed to Cristobal Balenciaga in Paris. 1961 opened own fashion house. Famous for minimal, silver and white space-age clothes, using innovative cutting and revolutionary materials including synthetics and new finishes.

COURTAULDS

Textile company founded England 1816 by Samuel Courtauld III as silk company.
Courtaulds USA founded 1911.
1905 first company to manufacture a regenerated cellulosic fibre, called viscose rayon, patented 1894 by Clayton Beadle,

Recuerdos de Nuestra Boda

A

EN EL DIA DE TU BODA

CON CARIÑO DE

PEGA AQUI UNA DE LAS TARJETAS DE INVITACION

Recuerdos de Nuestra Boda

Compilado por Sandra Carter

EDITORIAL
UNILIT

Publicado por
Editorial **Unilit**
Miami, Fl. EE.UU

Primera edición 1991

Texto ©1991 Lion Publishing
Originalmente publicado en inglés por
Lion Publishing plc, ©1991 Oxford, England
con el título: *Our Wedding: A Keepsake Album*
Todos los derechos reservados

Compilación ©1991 Sandra Carter
Ilustraciónes © 1991 Tessa Jackson
Traducido al español: Moisés N. Ramos

Reconocimientos:
Rita F. Snowden, oración tomada de *A Woman's Book of Prayers*,
es reproducido con permiso de Collins Publishers. Joyce Huggett,
cita tomada de *Two Into One,* y usada con permiso de Inter-Varsity Press.
Walter Trobisch, *I Married You.* es usado con permiso de Inter-Varsity Press.

Impreso en Italia
Producto 497605

ISBN 1-56063-162-7

INTRODUCCION

*El día de nuestra boda: un frenesí de actividad, un murmullo de emoción,
viejos amigos, lágrimas de madre, flores, besos, el pánico de última hora,
regalos, el pastel que hay que partir, ceremonia solemne,
bromas espontáneas.*

*Un día que puede comenzar en la familiaridad de mi vieja cama en casa,
y terminar lejos compartiendo una nueva vida.*

*En medio de todo el torbellino, damos hoy un paso de profunda significación.
Porque el día de nuestra boda es el primer día de nuestra vida de casados.
Le decimos adiós a nuestra vida de solteros y unimos nuestras manos
para iniciar un viaje juntos.*

*Es un viaje de compañerismo, en el cual se dividen los problemas y se duplican
las alegrías al abrazar el futuro juntos.*

*Es un viaje de descubrimiento, en el que el amor en acción profundiza nuestra
apreciación del uno por el otro a través de toda la vida.*

*Es un viaje de compartir, en el cual el hogar y los ratos libres, el trabajo y las
posesiones, las grandes decisiones, los pequeños secretos, los problemas
y los placeres ya no son "míos" sino "nuestros".*

*Es un viaje de fe, en el que entregamos todo lo que tenemos y somos el uno
al otro, y confiamos en Dios, quien planeó el matrimonio, para que nos
ayude a crecer en atención y deleite mutuos.*

*Nuestra relación, nuestro hogar, nuestra familia se edifican sobre las promesas
que se hacen hoy cuando ambos decimos, de lo profundo de
nuestros corazones: "Sí".*

NUESTRO DIA
ESPECIAL

Nuestro matrimonio se celebró en

Fecha

_____

Hora

_____

Lugar

_____

_____

La ceremonia fue oficiada por

_____

PEGA AQUI UNA FOTOGRAFIA DE LA NOVIA Y EL NOVIO

*G*racias por tu dulce y misterioso don
de amor; por todo lo que hallamos el
uno en el otro que nos atrae y enriquece.
Haz que nuestra relación comience en tu
presencia, alegrada por familiares y amigos
reunidos este día dentro de la iglesia, y que
sea fuerte, santa e imperecedera. Bendice
el hogar que planeamos construir y mantener
juntos. Que sus puertas estén siempre
abiertas a lo bueno, lo bello y lo que da gozo.
Permítenos amarnos y confiar en ti en tal
luz que si alguna vez los cielos se oscurecen
sobre nosotros, sepamos cuán cerca estás y
cuán amable y confiable eres.

RITA SNOWDEN

LA FIESTA
DE BODA

*No es amor el que
se altera cuando
encuentra alteración,
O tiende a cambiar al
presentarse cambios;
Oh ¡no! es un pilar
inconmovible, al que los
embates de la tempestad
nunca estremecen;
Es la estrella que guía a
cada barco extraviado, el
valor de la cual se desconoce,
aunque se aprecie su
altura.*

WILLIAM SHAKESPEARE

La novia usó

_____

_____

El novio usó

_____

La corte de la novia fueron

_____

_____

Ellos usaron

_____

_____

El padrino y la madrina fueron

_____

_____

Tú puedes dar sin amar,
pero no puedes amar
sin dar.

AMY CARMICHAEL

PEGA AQUI UNA FOTOGRAFIA
DE LA FIESTA DE LA BODA

¿*C*uál es el amor puro?
Aquel que siempre da
y nunca exige.

EVELYN UNDERHILL

LOS MOMENTOS
NOTABLES DEL DIA

Momentos o incidentes especiales
acaecidos durante el día que serán
inolvidables para nosotros.

*P adre celestial, te damos
gracias de que en nuestra
vida terrenal tú nos hablas de tu
vida eterna: rogamos que a través
de su matrimonio este hombre y
esta mujer te lleguen a conocer
mejor, amarte más y seguirte más
de cerca día por día.*

THE ALTERNATIVE SERVICE
BOOK 1980.

De ella

_____

_____

_____

_____

*E l matrimonio... de dos
vidas fraccionadas hace
un todo; le da una tarea a dos
vidas que no tenían propósito, y
duplica la fuerza de ambas para
que la realicen; concede a dos
naturalezas interrogantes una
razón para la vida, y a veces para
vivir; dará nueva alegría a la luz
del sol, nueva fragancia a las
flores, belleza nueva a la tierra y
un nuevo misterio a la vida.*

MARK TWAIN

De él

_____

_____

_____

_____

PEGA AQUI UNA FOTOGRAFIA
DEL RAMO DE LA NOVIA O
FIJA FLORES PRENSADAS DEL
ARREGLO FLORAL

Para conservar flores de tu ramo de novia como recuerdo:

Selecciona flores pequeñas, o toma pétalos de las grandes. Incluye algún helecho u otros de los componentes verdes.

Pon las flores que deseas prensar entre hojas de papel absorbente; coloca flores de un solo tipo en cada camada, de otro modo la presión no será uniforme.

Coloca papel de periódicos entre las distintas camadas de papel absorbente.

Comprímelas entre objetos pesados (libros grandes pueden servir) por varias semanas

Distribuye las flores prensadas en una lámina de cartulina, y emplea una cantidad reducida de goma de pegar para fijarlas.

Cubre la tarjeta con material plástico adhesivo transparente.

YO TE ACEPTO...

Estos son los votos que hicimos:

Las palabras de ella

_____

_____

_____

_____

Las palabras de él

_____

_____

_____

_____

E l amor no es el sentimiento de un momento,
sino la decisión consciente para una forma de vida.

ULRICH SCHAFFER

¿ *Q* ué prometías cuando intercambiabas votos?
¿Prometías sentir amor romántico por
siempre? Es claro que los votos matrimoniales no
pueden basarse en algo tan fugaz como los
sentimientos, porque, como dijo C.S. Lewis, 'nadie
puede prometer continuar sintiendo de cierta
manera. Porque sería lo mismo que prometer que
nunca va a tener un dolor de cabeza, que siempre
va a sentir hambre'.

E ntonces ¿qué estás prometiendo? Estás
pactando un amor que es más que un
sentimiento. Se mantiene por la voluntad. Tiene
que ver con acciones. Incluye cariño, apoyo y
atención del uno hacia el otro. Se trata de lealtad,
de compartir... Es cuestión de ayudarse el uno al
otro a ser lo mejor que podemos ser. Dios es amor,
y Su institución del matrimonio se caracteriza
por amor en acción.

JOYCE HUGGETT

M ejores son dos que uno; porque juntos
pueden trabajar más efectivamente.
Si uno de ellos cayere, el otro puede ayudarle a
levantarse.

ECLESIASTES 4:9-10

NUESTRA CEREMONIA
MATRIMONIAL

A labado sea Dios, que ha creado el noviazgo y el matrimonio, el gozo y la alegría, la celebración y la risa, el placer y el deleite, el amor, la hermandad, la paz y el compañerismo.

LIBRO DE CEREMONIAS METODISTA

Q ueremos hacer que nuestro matrimonio sea un éxito. Pero quizás necesitaremos alguna ayuda para poder vivir felizmente durante toda la vida. Por lo tanto, si el matrimonio es una dádiva tuya, te suplicamos, oh Dios, que nos muestres el camino que hemos de seguir, y que nos acompañes en nuestro viaje.

MARION STROUD

PEGA AQUI UNA DE LAS FOTOGRAFIAS
TOMADAS EN LA IGLESIA

PEGA AQUI EL PROGRAMA DE LA CEREMONIA O ESCRIBELO

EL
FESTEJO FAMILIAR

En Africa en algunos casos el cortejo nupcial danza, a veces por muchos kilómetros, desde la aldea de la novia hasta la del novio. No hay nada secreto en ello. Este acto público de la partida legaliza a la vez el matrimonio. Desde ese día en adelante todos lo saben: estos dos son esposo y esposa... Nunca el matrimonio es un asunto privado. No hay matrimonio sin boda. Por esta razón los matrimonios muchas veces se celebran con una gran fiesta.

WALTER TROBISCH

La recepción tuvo lugar en

_____

_____

Los discursos fueron pronunciados por

_____

_____

_____

Expresiones memorables en los discursos

_____

_____

_____

_____

EL MENU

PEGA UNA COPIA DEL MENU O ESCRIBELO

LOS INVITADOS
A LA BODA

Estuvieron presentes como testigos de nuestro
matrimonio y para celebrar con nosotros los
familiares y amigos siguientes:

PIDELE A LOS INVITADOS QUE FIRMEN ESTA PAGINA EN LA RECEPCION DE LA BODA

LA UNION DE
DOS FAMILIAS

Lágrimas de una madre

*Si lloro en este, el más especial de
    todos los días,
    son*
*Lágrimas de admiración por el
    maravilloso plan de Dios de crear
    un nuevo hogar de corazones
    amorosos*
*Lágrimas llenas de recuerdos del
    día que naciste, el gozo que
    trajiste a nuestra familia*
*Lágrimas de gozo porque hallaste
    al compañero de tu alma*
*Lágrimas de despedida, al cederte
    a tu acompañante*
*Lágrimas de oración del corazón
    que ruega que a través del viaje
    de la vida os traigáis el uno
    al otro grande gozo.*

SANDRA CARTER

PEGA AQUI UNA FOTOGRAFIA DE LA FAMILIA DEL NOVIO

PEGA AQUI UNA FOTOGRAFIA DE LA FAMILIA DE LA NOVIA

L a dádiva de Dios es vida eterna
ROMANOS 6:23

LOS REGALOS DE BODA

Nombre de la persona	Regalo que hizo	Se le envió carta de agradecimiento

Nombre de la persona   Regalo que hizo   Se le envió carta de agradecimiento

NUESTRA
LUNA DE MIEL

*'Llegar a ser una sola carne'
significa mucho más que la
mera unión física. Quiere decir que
dos personas comparten todo lo que
tienen, no únicamente sus cuerpos, no
sólo sus posesiones materiales, sino
también su manera de pensar y de
sentir, su gozo y sufrimiento, sus
esperanzas y temores, sus éxitos y sus
fracasos. 'Llegar a ser una sola carne'
significa que dos personas se transfor-
man totalmente en una en cuerpo,
alma y espíritu, y todavía siguen
siendo dos personas distintas. Este es
el misterio más secreto del matrimonio.
Es el más difícil de entender. Puede
ser que en manera alguna seamos
capaces de entenderlo. Podemos
sólo experimentarlo...*

WALTER TROBISCH

Pasamos nuestra luna de miel en

_____

_____

Adónde fuimos, qué vimos

_____

_____

_____

Nuestros recuerdos favoritos

_____

_____

_____

PEGA AQUI ALGUNAS DE TUS FOTOGRAFICAS FAVORITAS DE LA LUNA DE MIEL

DESDE HOY EN ADELANTE

Matrimonio.... dos personas que regalan por completo sus vidas el uno al otro, como si se dieran recíprocamente la facultad ilimitada de crecer con ayuda mutua.

ROBERT RUNCIE,
OBISPO DE CANTERBURY

Aunque éste sea el más humilde, ¡no hay lugar como el hogar!

JOHN HOWARD PAYNE (1791-1852)

Nuestro primer hogar estuvo ubicado en

_____

_____

_____

Nuestros primeros huéspedes fueron

_____

_____

_____

A n i v e r s a r i o s

1 PAPEL	**2** ALGODON	**3** CUERO	**4** FRUTA	
5 MADERA	**6** HIERRO	**7** LANA	**8** BRONCE	
9 CERAMICA	**10** LATA	**11** ACERO	**12** SEDA	
13 ENCAJE	**14** MARFIL	**15** CRISTAL	**20** PORCELANA	**25** PLATA
30 PERLA	**35** CORAL	**40** RUBI	**45** SAFIRO	**50** ORO
60 PLATINO	**75** DIAMANTE			

El amor es muy paciente y amable,
nunca celoso o envidioso,
nunca jactancioso u orgulloso,
nunca altanero, egoísta o rudo.
El amor no impone su propia voluntad.
No es irritable o quisquilloso.
No abriga resentimientos, y cuando otros
proceden mal apenas lo tomará en cuenta.
Nunca se alegra de la injusticia,
sino que se regocija siempre que triunfa la verdad.
Si amas a alguien
le serás leal a toda costa.
Siempre le creerás,
siempre esperarás lo mejor de él,
y siempre estarás dispuesto a defenderle...
El amor continúa para siempre.

1 CORINTIOS 13:4-8